IF THIS / THEN THAT

by Teddy Borth

Cody Koala

An Imprint of Pop!
popbooksonline.com

abdobooks.com

Published by Pop!, a division of ABDO, PO Box 398166, Minneapolis, Minnesota 55439. Copyright © 2022 by Abdo Consulting Group, Inc. International copyrights reserved in all countries. No part of this book may be reproduced in any form without written permission from the publisher. Cody Koala™ is a trademark and logo of Pop!.

Printed in the United States of America, North Mankato, Minnesota

052021
092021

THIS BOOK CONTAINS RECYCLED MATERIALS

Cover Photo: Shutterstock Images
Interior Photos: Shutterstock Images, 4, 9, 10; iStockphotos, 6 (top), 6 (bottom left and center), 6 (bottom right), 13, 15, 19, 21; Andre Jenny/Alamy Stock Photo, 16

Editor: Elizabeth Andrews
Series Designer: Laura Graphenteen

Library of Congress Control Number: 2020948284

Publisher's Cataloging-in-Publication Data

Names: Borth, Teddy, author.
Title: If this / then that / by Teddy Borth
Description: Minneapolis, Minnesota : Pop!, 2022 | Series: Coding basics | Includes online resources and index.
Identifiers: ISBN 9781532169649 (lib. bdg.) | ISBN 9781098240578 (ebook)
Subjects: LCSH: Conditionals (Logic)--Juvenile literature. | Application software--Juvenile literature. | Computer programming--Juvenile literature.
Classification: DDC 005.1--dc23

Hello! My name is

Cody Koala

Pop open this book and you'll find QR codes like this one, loaded with information, so you can learn even more!

Scan this code* and others like it while you read, or visit the website below to make this book pop.

popbooksonline.com/this-that

*Scanning QR codes requires a web-enabled smart device with a QR code reader app and a camera.

Table of Contents

Chapter 1

Checking Outcomes

A computer can't really see what is happening. It checks if specific things are true or false. **Coders** have to plan ahead. They think of every **outcome** and provide instructions.

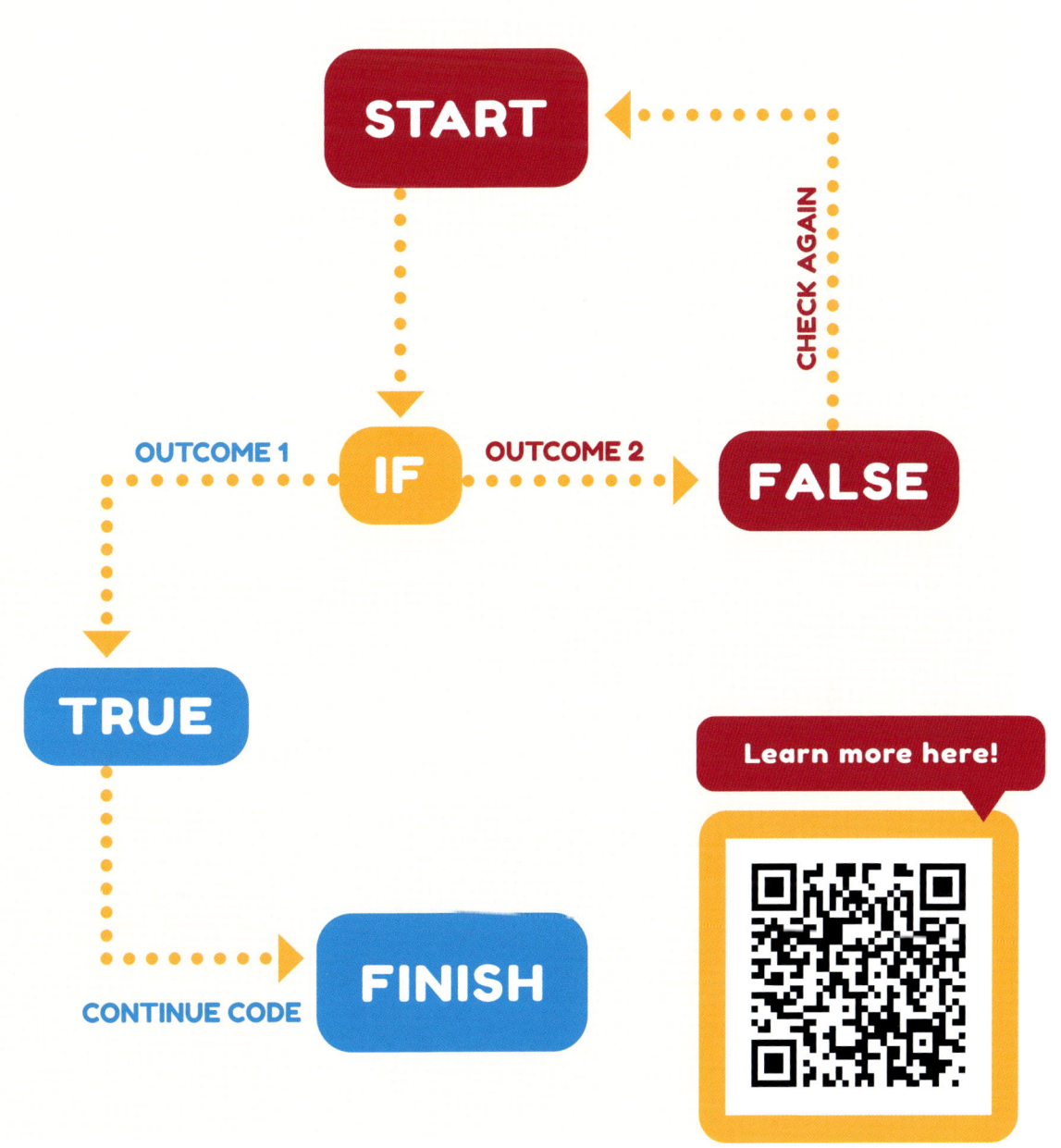

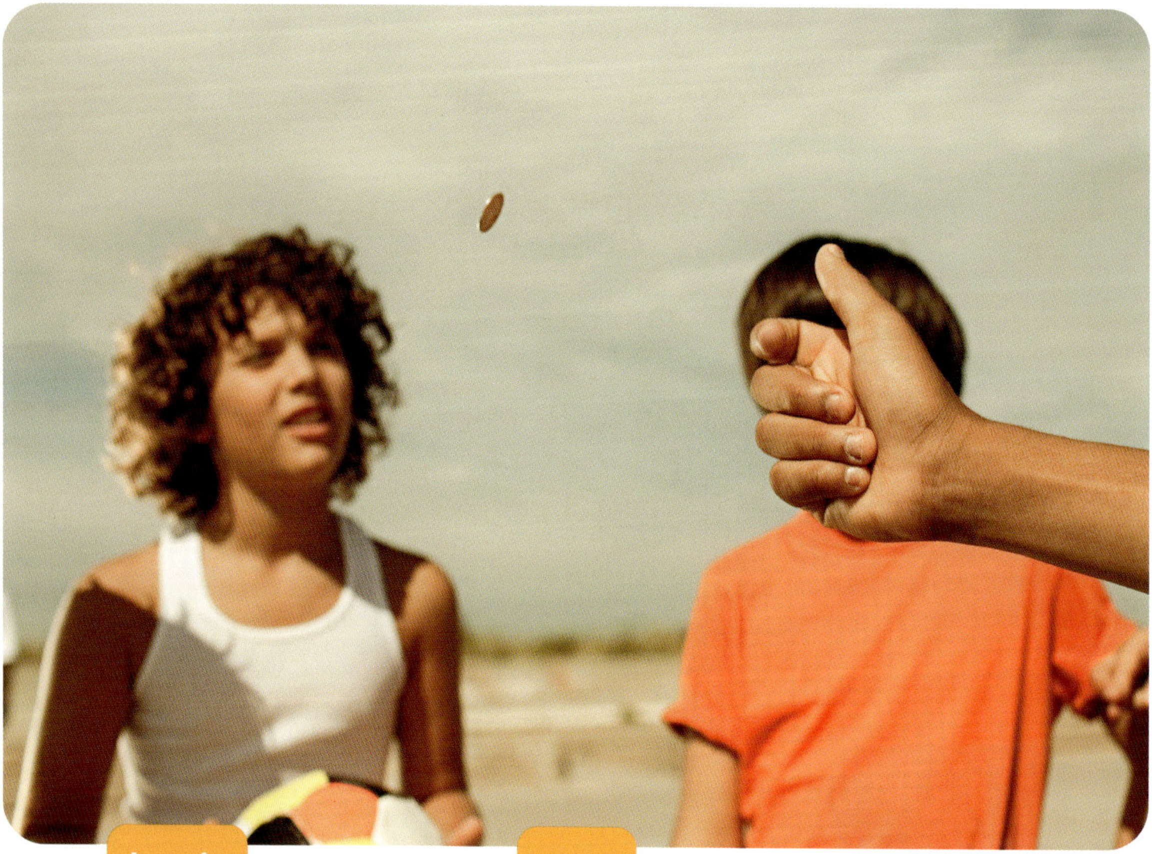

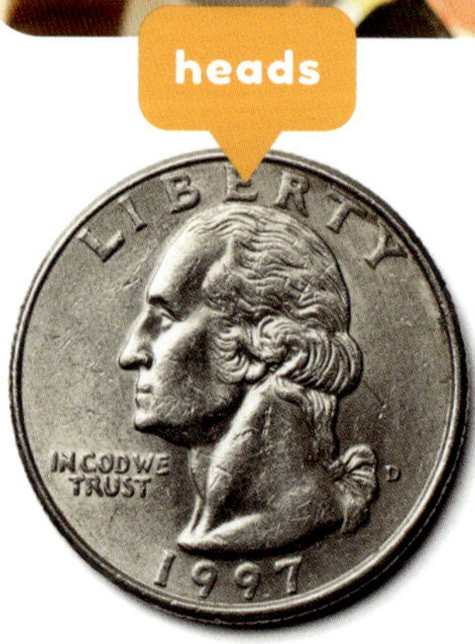
heads
LIBERTY
IN GOD WE TRUST
1997
D

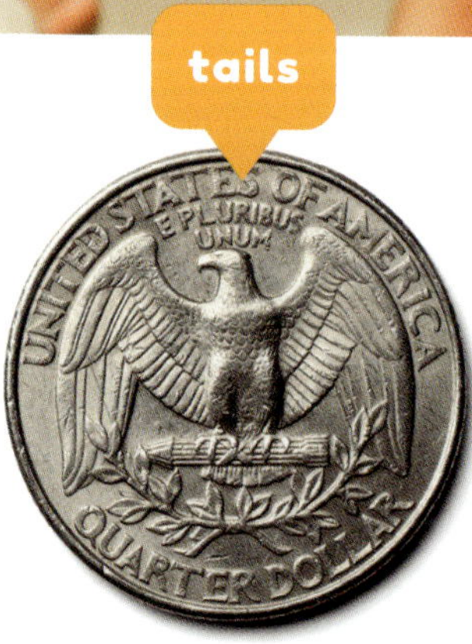
tails
UNITED STATES OF AMERICA
E PLURIBUS UNUM
QUARTER DOLLAR

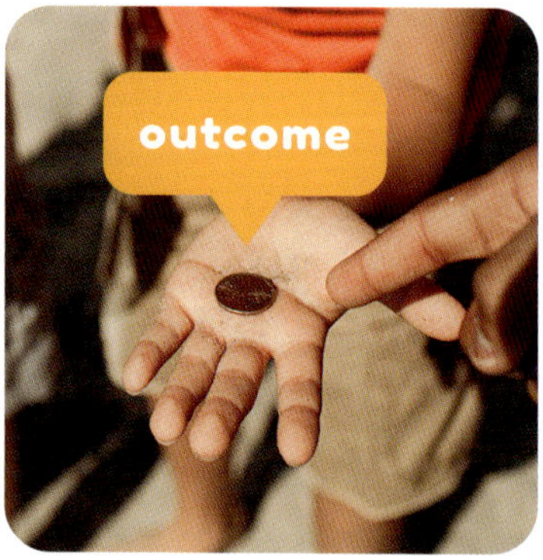
outcome

If a computer flips a coin, it doesn't know the result. It checks for outcomes one-by-one. It checks until it finds one that is true. It first looks if the coin landed on heads. If it didn't, it knows it must be tails. There are only two outcomes to look for.

Chapter 2

Making Decisions

Humans do this all the time. We check around us, then we perform a task. Tom is eating pizza. If he is still hungry, then he will get another slice. This **loop** continues until he is full.

Complete an activity here!

signal

Scott wants to walk across the street. He has to keep checking the crosswalk signal. If it is a don't walk signal, he has to wait. If it is a walk signal, then he can safely cross.

The first crossing signal was in London in 1868. A police officer had to crank it by hand.

Sometimes you have lots of things to check. Many if/then statements can be put together. Rhea checks the weather. If it is cold, then she wears a sweater. If it is cold *and* windy, then she wears a jacket too. If it is warm, then she wears neither.

Chapter 3

Look and React

Athletes have to always check what is happening. This helps them **react** and play. If they are losing, the athlete may take more risks in the game.

Watch a Video Here!

baserunner

batter

Like a **coder**, baseball coaches give instructions to baserunners. First, they check if the ball is hit. Then they check two more things. If it is a pop fly, they wait to see if it is caught. If it is a **ground ball**, they tell the baserunner to go!

The baseball **code** can get more complex. Players check how many outs there are. They also check on any **force outs** that could happen. All these checks change what players do when a ball is hit.

An athlete has to make on-the-fly decisions in every sport. These are all if/then statements that run very fast in the athlete's brain.

Chapter 4

If This,
Then That

Sara checks the calendar.

She needs to know what day

it is. The day tells her what

books she needs for school.

She is performing an if/then

check like a computer!

Learn more here!

Making Connections

Text-to-Self

What is your favorite sport to play? If the game isn't at your house, then how do you get there? If you win or lose, then how do you react?

Text-to-Text

Have you read other books that have "if this, then that" concepts? What did you learn?

Text-to-World

Think about weather around the world. If it is hot or cold outside, then what do people wear or do? If a blizzard or hurricane is in the forecast, then how do people prepare?

Glossary

code – a list of instructions that tells a computer what to do.

coder – a person who builds programs or works with computer languages.

force out – in baseball, a play in which a player can tag a base while holding the ball to cause the baserunner to be out.

ground ball – in baseball, a ball that is hit toward the ground.

loop – actions that repeat until stopped by something.

outcome – a result of something.

react – to move or act in response to something.

Index

Online Resources

popbooksonline.com

Thanks for reading this Cody Koala book!

Scan this code* and others like it in this book, or visit the website below to make this book pop!

popbooksonline.com/this-that

*Scanning QR codes requires a web-enabled smart device with a QR code reader app and a camera.